EDUCATOR'S NOTE

Dear Parents,

Welcome to the Scholastic Read and Learn Reader series. We have taken more than 80 years of experience with teachers, parents, and children and put it into a program that is designed to match your child's interests and skills.

- Look at the book together. Encourage your child to read the title and make a prediction about the story.

- Read the book together. Encourage your child to sound out words when appropriate. When your child struggles, you can help by providing the word.

- Encourage your child to retell the story. This is a great way to check for comprehension.

Scholastic Readers are designed to support your child's efforts to learn how to read at every age and every stage. Enjoy helping your child learn to read and love to read.

—*Francie Alexander*
Chief Education Officer
Scholastic Education

Jesus was blessed by God.
"You are my own dear Son," God said.

Jesus lived in a town in the land of Galilee. God told Jesus to teach the people of Galilee about the Kingdom of Heaven.

People came from far and near to hear Jesus talk about God. He blessed them and brought them much joy.

Then Jesus went out to teach the word of God to people in other places.

Jesus came to a town. He saw ten men.
They were all sick with a terrible disease.
The men had heard about Jesus. They
cried out, "Teacher, please help us."

Jesus blessed the ten men.

The men felt their bodies grow strong.
They were so happy! They ran off.
One man stopped. He turned around.

The man ran back to Jesus. He fell to his knees. "Thank you," he cried.

Jesus told the man to stand up. "Go home," he said. "Your faith in God has made you well."

Jesus walked on. He came to another town.

The people ran up to welcome him.

They wanted Jesus to bless their children.

Some men told them to go away. They said that Jesus didn't have time for children.

Jesus heard them. He said, "Let the children come to me!"

The children ran over to Jesus. He took them in his arms. He placed his hands on their heads and blessed them.

"The Kingdom of Heaven belongs to people who are like these little children," he said. "Don't stop them from coming to me."

Jesus stopped at the house of his
friend Martha.

She asked him to come in and eat.

Martha's sister Mary was there. She sat down to listen to Jesus.

Martha was working hard in the kitchen.
She wanted Mary to come and help her.

Martha went to get Mary. But Jesus said, "Let Mary stay. She is learning about God's kingdom. That is the best work she can do."

Jesus went on his way. Crowds of people followed him.

Everyone wanted to see him and hear him speak about God.

A blind man was sitting at the side of the road.

"What is happening?" he asked.

Someone said, "Jesus is coming!"

The blind man had heard about Jesus and all the good things he had done.

He called out in a loud voice, "Jesus, have pity on me!"

Jesus stopped. He asked the man, "What do you want me to do for you?"

"I want to see!" the man answered.

Jesus told him, "Look and you will see! Your eyes are healed because of your faith in God."

The man opened his eyes. He stood up and looked around. He saw Jesus. He saw the sun shining. He saw the bright colors of the clothes people were wearing.

The people shouted, "Praise be to God."

Now the man could do anything he wanted. But he wanted to do only one thing. He wanted to go with Jesus. And he did.

Do you know . . .

. . . that Galilee (page 6) was the region between the Mediterranean Sea on the west and the Jordan River and the Sea of Galilee on the east in Roman times?

. . . that in Jesus's time teachers sat down when they taught? The people sat in a semicircle and faced the teacher (page 7).

. . . that a disciple is someone who learns from a teacher?

. . . that an apostle is someone who is sent to teach others?

. . . that Bethany is the name of the village where Martha and Mary lived? It is located about two miles east of Jerusalem, on the slopes of the Mount of Olives.